Ex

Vulnerable People
to Euthanasia and Assisted Suicide

"Using already existing studies, Schadenberg has uncovered the shocking truth about euthanasia in Belgium, the lives lost and the deep threat to others. His work demonstrates unequivocally that we must never follow this Belgian pathway to the easy killing of people whose lives are not valued by those who do the killing."

Kevin Fitzpatrick, Not Dead Yet, UK

"Alex Schadenberg has done the debate on euthanasia and assisted suicide a great service in this comprehensive work. His thorough-going analysis of the available studies concerning The Netherlands and Belgium demand a response from those who support euthanasia & assisted suicide. This work supports empirically the observation that no legislation can ever protect all citizens from the possibility of abuse. For legislators and commentators alike, this is a must read."

Paul Russell, President of HOPE Australia

"My friend was diagnosed with pancreas cancer in 2011. He had to turn down three independent euthanasia suggestions by his attending physicians. The suggestions were against our liberal euthanasia laws. It proves our societies are indeed on "a slippery slope" as argumented in this study; it's high time to wake up, we may already have passed the point of no return. Schadenberg conclusive remark therefore should be taken seriously."

Michael van der Mast, Cry for life - Netherlands

Library and Archives Canada Cataloguing in Publication

Schadenberg, Alex, 1968-, author
   Exposing vulnerable people to euthanasia and assisted suicide / Alex Schadenberg.
   Includes bibliographical references.
   Issued in print and electronic formats.
   ISBN 978-1-4922-0041-3
   1. Euthanasia--Belgium. 2. Assisted suicide--Belgium. 3. Euthanasia--Netherlands. 4. Assisted suicide--Netherlands.
   I. Euthanasia Prevention Coalition
   II. Title.

R726.S34 2013   179.7   C2013-904556-2
                                              C2013-904557-0

Alex Schadenberg can be contacted at: info@epcc.ca

Website: www.epcc.ca

or Phone: 1-877-439-3348.

Published in Canada by:

Ross Lattner Educational Consultants

Euthanasia Prevention Coalition

PO Box 2503, London, ON Canada N6C 6A8

or

PO Box 611309 Port Huron MI USA 48061-1309

Cover image "Female Doctor With Syringe" by Ambro. (FreeDigitalPhotos.net)

Alex Schadenberg has been the executive director of the Euthanasia Prevention Coalition (EPC) since its founding in 1998. Alex is known for his research into issues related to euthanasia, assisted suicide and other end-of-life issues and concerns. This is the second book that has been written by Alex.

Alex's articles have been published throughout the world and his blog (www.alexschadenberg.blogspot.com) has become known as a definitive source of information on issues related to euthanasia and assisted suicide.

He is also a world renowned speaker and has spoken throughout Canada, the United States, Australia, New Zealand, Scotland, Switzerland and Italy.

In November 2007 he was chosen as the Chair of the Euthanasia Prevention Coalition - International, a co-ordinating body of groups that work to oppose euthanasia and assisted suicide.

Dr. Barrie DeVeber and Alex Schadenberg

Alex works with many other groups to establish an effective world-wide opposition to euthanasia and assisted suicide, such as: HOPE Australia, TAS, Choice is an Illusion, and the Care Not Killing Alliance.

Alex organized:

The First International Symposium on Euthanasia and Assisted Suicide (November 30 - December 1, 2007) in Toronto Ontario.

The Second International Symposium on Euthanasia and Asssisted Suicide (May 29 - 30, 2009) near Washington DC.

The Third International Symposium on Euthanasia and Assisted Suicide (June 3 - 4, 2011) in Vancouver BC.

Alex also helped to organize:

The First European Symposium on Euthanasia and Assisted Suicide (Sept 7 - 8, 2012) in Edinburgh Scotland.

Alex is married to Susan and they have six children.

Contents

Background

In the past few years, several reports have been written by euthanasia proponents claiming that vulnerable patient groups are not adversely affected by legalizing euthanasia or assisted suicide. These reports have concluded that there is no evidence that vulnerable people are threatened by legalizing euthanasia or assisted suicide and there is no evidence of a "slippery slope."

This document is a response to these reports and to the key characteristics they share in common. I will demonstrate that:

i. The studies used to determine that there is no proof that vulnerable patient groups are negatively affected by the legalization of euthanasia are based on a pre-conceived outcome rather than openly considered the issues.[1]

ii. The conclusions of these studies are based on selective data.

iii. When one analyzes the data concerning euthanasia deaths without request and the unreported euthanasia deaths, one comes to a different conclusion.

This book proves that the conclusions of the *Royal Society of Canada End-of-Life Decision Making report*, the *Quebec government Select Committee on Dying with Dignity report*, the *Commission on Assisted Dying in the UK* and the decision by Justice Lynn Smith in *Carter v. Attorney General of Canada* are false and misleading. The studies that these reports base their conclusions upon, are not supported by the data.

The Terms of Reference:

Euthanasia is an action or omission of an action that is done to directly and intentionally cause the death of another person to end suffering. Euthanasia is a form of homicide that is usually done by lethal injection. To legalize euthanasia, a nation would be required to create an exception to homicide in its criminal code. It is sometimes referred to as "Mercy Killing."

Assisted suicide is a death in which one person aids, counsels or encourages another person to commit suicide. Assisted suicide usually occurs when a physician prescribes a lethal dose to a person, knowing that the person intends to use the lethal dose for the purpose of suicide. It is sometimes referred to as physician-prescribed suicide.

Euthanasia and assisted suicide are similar since both require another person to be directly and intentionally involved with causing the death of another person. However, euthanasia and assisted suicide differ based on who completes the act.

Euthanasia and assisted suicide are direct and intentional. Therefore, the proper use of large doses of pain-killing drugs (analgesics), the proper use of sedation techniques oriented to eliminating pain and the withdrawing of medical treatment do not constitute euthanasia or assisted suicide.

In Canada, and many other countries such as Australia, New Zealand, France and the United Kingdom (UK), there is a strong societal debate occurring concerning the legalization of euthanasia. In the United States there is a societal debate occurring concerning the legalization of assisted suicide.

Nature of the Research:

This document will prove that if a researcher only focuses on the data from the reported euthanasia deaths or the "official statistics," it will appear that vulnerable groups are not adversely affected by the legalization of euthanasia. It will also appear that there are very few, if any, problems with the implementation of euthanasia laws and no fear of a "slippery slope."

If a researcher analyzes the unreported cases of euthanasia or the euthanasia deaths that are done without explicit request, in Belgium, then the research uncovers proof that vulnerable patient groups are adversely affected by the legalization of euthanasia or assisted suicide.

The studies from Belgium also uncover other abuse of the euthanasia procedure, such as euthanasia by nurses, little protection for depressed people or people with mental illness, et cetera.

The abuse that occurs with the implementation of euthanasia that the studies uncover shows that statements such as: there are no fears of a "slippery slope" are false or misleading at best.

Medical End-of-Life Practices Under the Euthanasia Law in Belgium

New England Journal of Medicine, September 10, 2009 [2]

This article summarizes a larger study concerning the practice of euthanasia and other medical end-of-life practices in Belgium. The article also reports on the rate of euthanasia deaths without an explicit request and the practice of deep-continuous sedation in Belgium. [3]

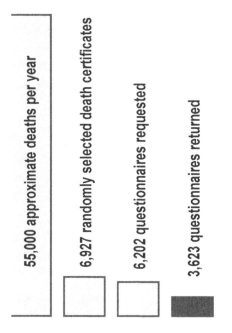

This is the first of three articles that are based on data from death certificates in the Flemish region of Belgium, a region with approximately 6 million people, representing 55,000 deaths per year. A random sample of 6,927 deaths from June 1 - November 30, 2007 were studied. A five-page questionnaire was sent to the certifying physician in each death to determine what occurred. 3,623 questionnaires were returned and no response was possible for 725 of the questionnaires, leaving a 58.4% response rate (3,623 of the 6,202 valid cases).[4] This article establishes the demographic group for those who die by euthanasia. The article states:

> *"We found no shift in the characteristics of patients whose death was the result of euthanasia (mostly younger patients with cancer, or patients dying at home) ... the characteristics of whom lethal drugs (euthanasia) were used without request or consent (mostly older, incompetent patients), patients with cardiovascular diseases or cancer; or patients dying in hospitals)."*[5]

The article determined that a significant number of euthanasia deaths occur in Belgium without explicit request. The article stated:

"In 1.8% of all deaths, lethal drugs were used without the patient's explicit request."[6]

Those who die by euthanasia without explicit request represent a different demographic group than those who die by euthanasia with explicit request.[7]

The article found that in 14.5% of all deaths in 2007 in Belgium, physicians reported using deep-continuous sedation until death, which represented an increase from a rate of 8.2% of all deaths from a study in 2001.[8]

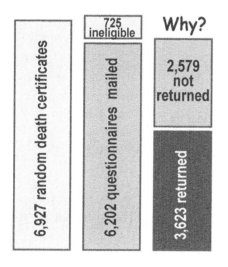

Deep-continuous sedation is usually done by sedating a person and then withdrawing all medical treatment and care including hydration and nutrition. It is sometimes referred to as terminal sedation.

Deep-continuous sedation can be ethically the same as euthanasia when it is done with the intention of causing the death of a person who is not otherwise dying, and when the cause of death is intentional dehydration.

A study published in *The Lancet*, entitled *"Trends in end-of-life practices before and after the enactment of the euthanasia law in the Netherlands from 1990 to 2010: a repeated cross-sectional survey,"*[9] concerns end-of-life practices in the Netherlands. This study found that the practice of deep-continuous sedation has risen dramatically since euthanasia became officially legal in the Netherlands in 2002. The study determined deep-continuous sedation was related to all deaths 5.6% of the time in 2001, 8.2% of the time in 2005 and 12.3% of the time in 2010 in the Netherlands.[10]

Therefore, Belgium and the Netherlands have both experienced a significant increase in the rate of deep-continuous sedation since the legalization of euthanasia.

Conclusion

This article is the first to state that a different demographic group exists for those who die by euthanasia without an explicit request than people who die by euthanasia with request.

People who die by euthanasia without an explicit request are:

"mostly older, incompetent patients; patients with cardiovascular diseases or cancer; or patients dying in hospitals."[11]

People who die by euthanasia with an explicit request are:

"mostly younger patients, patients with cancer or patients dying at home."[12]

The article concluded that:

"We found that the enactment of the Belgium euthanasia law was followed by an increase in all types of medical end-of-life practices. ... However, the substantial increase in the frequency of deep sedation demands more in-depth research."[13]

Similar to the Netherlands, the massive increase in use of deep-continuous sedation suggests that it may be abused. The abuse of deep-continuous sedation needs to be further studied.

Physician-Assisted Deaths Under the Euthanasia Law in Belgium: A Population-Based Survey

Canadian Medical Association Journal, *June 15, 2010* [14]

A random sample of 6,927 deaths from June 1 to November 30, 2007 were analysed within the study. The researchers sent a five-page questionnaire to the certifying physician in each of the deaths to determine what occurred. The researchers received 3,623 responses, while no response was possible for 725 of the questionnaires, a 58.4% response rate. [15]

This study is the second of three articles based on data from death certificates in the Flanders region of Belgium. Based on the 3,623 responses, the researchers identified that there were 137 euthanasia deaths, 5 assisted suicide deaths and 66 assisted deaths without explicit request.[16] Therefore there were 208 assisted deaths with 66 (32%) of the assisted deaths being done without explicit request. The study indicated that most of the people who die without explicit request were not competent. The study stated:

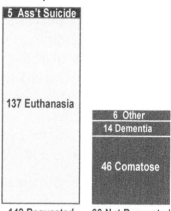

208 Reported Assisted Deaths

5 Ass't Suicide

137 Euthanasia

6 Other
14 Dementia
46 Comatose

142 Requested   66 Not Requested

"Where the decision had not been discussed with the patient, the physician specified as reason(s) that the patient was comatose (70.1% of the cases) or had dementia (21.1% of the cases); in 40.4% of the cases, the physician indicated that the patient had previously expressed a wish for ending life (not equivalent to an explicit request for euthanasia)." [17]

Most of the euthanasia deaths without explicit request were done to people who did not, and could not, request euthanasia at the time of death.

The study indicated that euthanasia without explicit request was only discussed with the patient in 22.1% of the cases.[18] Some of the reasons physicians did not discuss euthanasia with the patients were: 17% of the time the physician thought it was in the best interest of the patient, while 8.2% of the time the physician thought the discussion itself would have been harmful.[19]

The study found that euthanasia with request was most often done to alleviate pain or to fulfill a wish to end life.[20] Euthanasia without explicit request was most often to reduce the burden on the family or because they did not want to needlessly prolong the life of the patient.[21]

Another difference between euthanasia with an explicit request and euthanasia without an explicit request was the length and goal of treatment. People who died by euthanasia with request were, on average, receiving treatment for their illness for more than six months and the goal of treatment in the last week of life was comfort care and not cure. People who died by euthanasia without an explicit request, on average, received treatment for one month; and they were more likely to have had a cure as their goal of treatment in the last week.[22]

The demographic group of patients euthanized without explicit request. "fits the description of vulnerable patient groups..."

Euthanasia with request was most often done by barbiturate and muscle relaxant. Euthanasia without explicit request was usually done by intentional overdose of opioids, giving a level higher than needed to alleviate the patient's symptoms.[23] The article also stated that nurses were more often involved in the administration of the drugs with euthanasia without explicit request.[24]

The research team found that the demographic group of persons who died by euthanasia with request in comparison to euthanasia without explicit request was different. The study states:

> *"Our finding that euthanasia and assisted suicide were typically performed in younger patients, patients with cancer and patients dying at home is consistent with findings from other studies. Our finding that the use of life-ending drugs*

*without explicit patient request occurred predominantly in hospital and among patients 80 years or older who were mostly in coma or had dementia **fits the description of "vulnerable" patient groups at risk of life-ending without request.** "*[25]

In their conclusion, the authors stated:

"Our study showed that physician-assisted death with an explicit request from the patient (euthanasia and assisted suicide) and use of life-ending drugs without an explicit request were different types of end-of-life decisions that occurred in different patient groups and under different circumstances. Unlike euthanasia and assisted suicide, the use of life-ending drugs without an explicit patient request often involved patients with diseases other than cancer, which have an unpredictable end-of-life trajectory."[26]

Previous studies in Belgium concerning the characteristics of reported euthanasia deaths described the demographic for euthanasia as:

"Men, younger patients, and cancer patients were significantly over-represented in euthanasia cases. Patients of 80 years or more were under-represented in all places of death among cancer and non-cancer patients."[27]

This study found that euthanasia without request represented a different demographic group from those who died by euthanasia with an explicit request. The study stated that for euthanasia deaths without an explicit request:

"most involved patients who were 80 years of age or older (52.7%), those without cancer (67.5%) and those who died in hospital (67.1%)."[28]

This fact that euthanasia deaths with request represented a different demographic group than euthanasia deaths without explicit request is important. Research reports that have been written by pro-euthanasia authors claim that there is no sign of risk for vulnerable groups in jurisdictions where euthanasia is legal.[29]

Previous studies did not include euthanasia deaths without request within their statistics because these deaths are less likely to be reported as compared to euthanasia deaths with request.[30]

Conclusion

People who die by euthanasia without explicit request are often incompetent to make medical decisions. The person often has chronic conditions where the end-of-life trajectory is unknown. It is the opinion of this author that physicians and nurses are, at times, reacting to pressure from families to "get on with the death" and they are reacting to pressures from the health care institution to contain costs by dealing with the problem of the "bed blocker."

The demographic group for those who die by euthanasia by request is a different demographic group of people from those who die by euthanasia without an explicit request. This demographic group "fits the description of vulnerable patient groups at risk of life-ending without request."[31]

The Role of Nurses in Physician-assisted Deaths in Belgium

Canadian Medical Association Journal, June 15, 2010 [32]

The purpose of this study was to examine the involvement of nurses in Flanders, Belgium, in the decision-making, the preparation, and in the administration of life-ending drugs with or without a patient's explicit request in Flanders, Belgium. [33]

This study was the second phase of a two-phase study conducted between August and November 2007. The first phase of the study involved 6,000 nurses in Flanders, Belgium who were asked their attitudes towards life-shortening end-of-life decisions. The response rate for the first phase of the study was 63%. In that survey, the researchers assessed the experience with end-of-life shortening in the past 12 months. [34]

The second phase of the study analyzed the results of the first phase and determined that 1,678 nurses fit the criteria for the second phase of the study. Between November 2007 and February 2008, the research team sent questionnaires with letters of support from two major professional nursing organizations to the 1,678 nurses. Confidentiality was ensured and all data was processed anonymously. [35]

Ten of the 1,678 questionnaires were returned as undeliverable and of the remaining 1,668, 1,265 of the questionnaires were returned as completed, representing a response rate of 76%. [36]

The responses from the questionnaire determined that 248 nurses reported that the last patient in their care died by euthanasia. Almost half (120 nurses) reported that the last patient in their care died by euthanasia without explicit request. [37] The study begins by stating:

"In Belgium, the law permits physicians to perform euthanasia under strict requirements of due care, one of which is that they must discuss the request with the nurses involved." [38]

The law in Belgium does not permit nurses to carry-out the act of euthanasia or to assist a suicide. [39]

Nurses who worked in a home care setting were more likely to be involved in cases of euthanasia with explicit request (25%) than cases of euthanasia without explicit request (10%). Nurses who worked in care homes (nursing homes) were more likely to be involved with cases of euthanasia without explicit request (27%) as opposed to euthanasia with explicit request (16%).[40]

This study also determined that people who died by euthanasia with request were more likely to

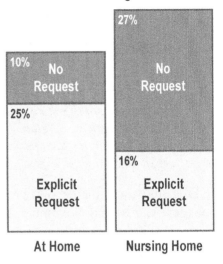

Nurses Administring Euthanasia

27%
No Request

10%
No Request

25%

16%

Explicit Request

Explicit Request

At Home   **Nursing Home**

be under the age of 80, to have cancer and to die at home. In contrast, people who died by euthanasia without explicit request were more likely to be over the age of 80, were less likely to have had cancer and were more likely to die in a hospital.[41] These findings are the same as the findings in the study "Physician-assisted deaths under the euthanasia law in Belgium: a population-based survey"[42] that found that 32% of all euthanasia deaths in the Flanders region of Belgium were done without explicit request.[43]

In cases where the patient died by euthanasia **with explicit request,** the patient had expressed their wish to the nurse 69% of the time, and the nurse reported being involved in the decision-making process 64% of the time. 40% of the nurses were involved in the preparation of the lethal dose, 34% of the nurses were present when the lethal dose was injected, and 31% of nurses provided support to the patient, the relatives, the physician or a fellow nurse.[44]

In cases where the patient died by euthanasia **without explicit request**, the patient had expressed their wish to the nurse 4% of the time, and the nurse reported being involved in the decision-making process 69% of the time. 48% of the nurses were involved in the preparation of the lethal dose, 56% of the nurses were present when the lethal dose was injected, and 51% of nurses provided support to the patient, the relatives, the physician or a fellow nurse.[45]

Euthanasia with request is often, but not always, discussed with the nurse; whereas euthanasia without explicit request was rarely discussed with the patient. The nurses are more likely to be directly involved in euthanasia when it is done without explicit request. The lethal dose was injected by the nurse 12% of the time, even though this is illegal. The study stated:

The lethal dose was injected by the nurse 12% of the time, even though this is illegal.

> *"The drugs were administered by the nurse in 14 (12%) of the cases of euthanasia. The physician was not co-administrator in 12 of the 14 cases, but the drug was always given on his or her orders. The nurse administered neuromuscular relaxant in four cases, a barbiturate in one case and opioids in nine cases. In nine cases the physician was not present during the administration of drugs."[46]*

The study also stated that the factors that were significantly associated with the nurse administering life-ending drugs were:

> *"the absence of an explicit request from the patient, the patient being more than 80 years old and the nurse having had a recent experience with life-shortening end-of-life decisions."[47]*

The study indicated other factors were associated with the nurse administering life-ending drugs:

> *"female nurses working in hospitals were six times and male nurses working in hospitals were forty times more likely than their male and female counterparts working in other settings to administer the life-ending drugs."[48]*

Therefore, nurses who have administered a euthanasia death are more likely to do it again and male nurses are far more likely to administer a lethal dose than female nurses.

Important Concerns:

The administration of life-ending drugs by nurses whether or not it is under the physicians' responsibility is not legal under the Belgian euthanasia law. This study found that the nurse injected the lethal dose into the patient in 12% of the euthanasia deaths that they were involved in and 45% of the euthanasia deaths were without explicit request.[49]

It must be noted that phase one of the study entitled *"Attitudes of nurses toward euthanasia and towards their role in euthanasia: a nationwide study in Flanders Belgium"* found that of the 6,000 nurses who participated, 57% of the nurses accepted using lethal drugs for patients who suffer unbearably and are not capable of making decisions.[50]

45% of euthanasia deaths administered by nurses were done without explicit patient request.

The study indicated that the law is not being followed. The study stated:

> *"It seems that the current law (which does not allow nurses to administer the life-ending drugs) and a control system do not prevent nurses from administering life-ending drugs."*[51]

The study acknowledged its limitations:

> *"Our study is possibly limited by selection bias, a reluctance of respondents to report illegal acts, the self-reported nature of the data and the lack of information from attending physicians or about the doses of drugs used."*[52]

The study found that nurses are acting outside of the law. The study states:

> *"By administering life-ending drugs at the physician's request in some cases of euthanasia, and even more so in cases without an explicit request from the patient, the nurses in our study operated beyond the legal margins of their profession."*[53]

The study warns that actions outside of the law could cause nurses problems:

> *"In particular, when criteria for due care are not fulfilled, such as in cases where the patient has not made an explicit request, nurses, next to the physician, risk legal prosecu-*

tion. Nurses may get caught in a vulnerable position between following a physician's orders and performing an illegal act. "[54]

Physicians in Belgium are required to report every euthanasia case. This study, regarding a previous study, concluded:

"In a study of all cases of euthanasia in Belgium, "Legal Euthanasia in Belgium: Characteristics of All Reported Euthanasia Cases," Journal of Medical Care,[55] Smets and colleagues found that physicians did not always report their cases and that unreported cases often involved the use of opioids and the administration of them by nurses.[56]

Conclusion:

Nurses in Belgium are participating in euthanasia with or without explicit consent, which is not legal under the Belgian euthanasia law. Even though nurses are usually not acting on their own, they are not discussing the decision with the patients.

Similar to the other studies, this study found that the demographic group that is dying without explicit consent is a different from the demographic group that dies with explicit consent.

Researchers Respond to the Study "Role of Nurses in Physician-Assisted Deaths in Belgium"

***Canadian Medical Association Journal**, June 23, 2010*

The fourth document analyzed is a challenge to the study entitled "The role of nurses in physician-assisted deaths in Belgium"[57] and the response by one of the authors of the study, defending the conclusion of the study.[58]

On June 23, 2010, the Canadian Medical Association Journal published "A Response to 'The role of nurses in physician-assisted deaths in Belgium,'[59] by Dr. Victor Cellarius, Temmy Latner Centre for Palliative Care, Mount Sinai Hospital, Toronto."[60]

Dr. Cellarius questioned whether the conclusion from the study "The role of nurses in physician-assisted deaths in Belgium" was accurate. Cellarius questioned that nearly half of the assisted deaths were done without explicit consent. He stated:

> "...the article shows in tabular form that of the 'unexplicitly requested' assisted deaths, nurses discussed the patient's or relatives' wishes in 41% of cases when they were involved in decision-making – why is this not mentioned in the text? In the other cases was the doctor involved? Or others? The nurse answering the questionnaire may not have known, but the interpretation suggested (or at least made by many) seems to be that no discussion was had. The article makes several important claims that describe evasion or overlooking of law and policy, but the most startling suggestion – that half of cases of assisted death are without consent – is the least supported. On this ground the article should be faulted for not making clear that the evidence does not permit such an interpretation."[61]

On June 30, 2010, the Canadian Medical Association Journal published the "Response to Victor Cellarius, ie: The role of nurses in physician-assisted deaths in Belgium, Els Inghelbrecht, End-of-Life Care Research Group, Vrije Universiteit Brussell,"[62] in which Dr. Inghelbrecht stated:

"In our article it is stated that half of cases of assisted death are performed without the patient's explicit request. This is very much supported by the data in the article. There was patient consent or a wish from the patient in some of these cases, but in the administration of life-ending drugs this is legally not a sufficient reason. Furthermore a request or wish from relatives acting as surrogate decision-makers is equally regarded as insufficient to justify such acts. ... The focus of our article was explicitly on the role of nurses in decision-making and in the preparation and administration of life-ending drugs in case of assisted death with and without explicit patient request. Our questionnaire indeed asked whether there was discussion between the nurse and the relatives in those cases – which happened in 68.9% – but we did not include this in our article because involving the relatives, especially in case of patient incompetence, is ultimately the responsibility of the physician, as is the decision itself. The decision is not made between nurses and relatives, but by the physician with input from relatives as well as nurses. "[63]

Conclusion:

The communication between Inghelbrecht and Cellarius confirms that the conclusion of the study that indicated 120 of 248 assisted deaths that nurses were directly involved with were done without explicit request is, in fact, accurate.

The communication also confirms that nurses are actually carrying-out acts of euthanasia, and this is outside of the legal practice of euthanasia in Belgium.

With respect to communication, Inghelbrecht confirmed that 68.9% of the time the relatives discussed the decision to cause death, but Inghelbrecht emphasized that this does not constitute an explicit request; and in Belgium, only physicians and not nurses have the responsibility to make such a decision.

Reporting of Euthanasia in Medical Practice in Flanders Belgium: Cross Sectional Analysis of Reported and Unreported Cases

British Medical Journal, *November 2010*[64]

This study concerns the reporting of euthanasia in the Flanders region of Belgium under the euthanasia law. It is the third of three studies based on data from death certificates in the Flanders region of Belgium. A random sample of 6,927 deaths from June 1 to November 30, 2007 was analyzed within the study. A five-page questionnaire was sent to the certifying physician in each of the deaths to determine what occurred. The researchers received 3,623 questionnaires while no response was possible for 725 of the questionnaires leaving a 58.4% response rate (3,623 of the 6,202 valid cases).[65]

Based on the responses from the 3,623 questionnaires, the study concluded 52.8% of the euthanasia deaths in the Flanders region of Belgium were reported, while 47.2% of the euthanasia deaths were unreported.[66]

> *"...concerns exist that only cases of euthanasia that are dealt with carefully are being reported."*

The study offers significant explanation into why euthanasia deaths are not being reported. The study found that the unreported euthanasia deaths were significantly different than the reported euthanasia deaths. The study stated:

> *"According to these documents, physicians who reported cases practised euthanasia carefully and in compliance with the law, and no cases of abuse have been found. However, concerns exist that only cases of euthanasia that are dealt with carefully are being reported."*[67]

The following reasons were offered by the doctors for not reporting a death as euthanasia:

"For 76.7% of the cases, physicians answered that they did not perceive their act as euthanasia, whereas for 17.9% they gave the reason that reporting is too much of an administrative burden, 11.9% that the legal due requirement

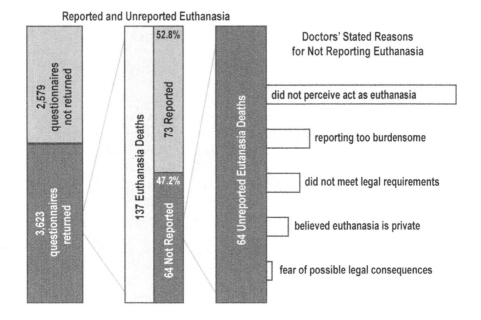

had possibly not all been met, and 9% that euthanasia is a private matter between the physician and patient (8.7%). A small proportion (2.3%) did not report the case because of possible legal consequences. "[68]

Similar to the Belgian study that determined that 32% of euthanasia deaths were without explicit request,[69] the unreported euthanasia deaths represented a different demographic group than the reported cases. The study stated:

> *"However, in a bivariate analysis there was a significant relation between reporting of euthanasia and the patient's age, with deaths of patients aged 80 years or older reported significantly less often than deaths of younger patients. Cases were also reported less often when the time by which life was shortened was less than one week compared with when the life shortening effect was greater. "*[70]

The issue of whether or not physicians ensured that the "safeguards" were followed or that the "due care" criteria was maintained is important. When the death was reported as euthanasia, usually the safeguards or due care criteria were followed, but when the death was not reported the "rules" were often not followed.

The study found that the difference between reported and unreported cases of euthanasia was:

> *"A verbal as well as a written request for euthanasia was present in 73.1% of all reported cases, whereas a legally required written request was absent in the majority (87.7%) of the unreported cases. In reported cases, the decision was always discussed with others, which was not always the case (85.2%) in unreported cases. Other physicians and care givers specialised in palliative care were consulted (97.5%) more often in reported cases than in unreported cases (54.6%). ... In reported cases of euthanasia the drugs were almost always administered by a physician (97.7%); in unreported cases, the drugs were often administered by a nurse alone (41.3%)."* [71]

This meant that the legal requirements for requesting euthanasia were met 73.1% of the time when the euthanasia death was reported. The legal requirements were met 12.3% of the time when the euthanasia death was unreported. A palliative care consultation was usually done when the euthanasia case was reported but a palliative care consultation was only **"...in unreported cases, the drugs were often administered by a nurse alone..."** done half the time when the euthanasia case was not reported. It is interesting that reported euthanasia cases were not always done by a physician, but more than half of the euthanasia deaths that were not reported were not done by a physician.

The strength of this study is based on the fact that the physicians self-reported the findings. A weakness in the study is that the findings were only based on the Flemish region of Belgium. It is believed that the French-speaking region of Belgium has a different attitude toward euthanasia than the Flemish region.[72]

The study offered several reasons for the high rate of unreported euthanasia deaths. The first being that the Flanders region of Belgium does not have a long-term experience with euthanasia, as compared to the Netherlands, who had a reporting procedure for many years before euthanasia was officially legalized in 2002.[73]

Many physicians did not realize that injecting a lethal dose of opioids with the intention of causing death is euthanasia. This also explains the large number of unreported euthanasia deaths that are done by nurses, which is illegal under the Belgian euthanasia law. Nurses are often administer opioids for palliative care and therefore when the intentional lethal overdose is "covered-up" as palliative care, it is not surprising that nurses administered the lethal dose.[74]

"... such legislation alone does not seem sufficient ... to guarantee the careful practice of euthanasia"

A second reason the study offered for the high rate of unreported euthanasia was that the physicians are more comfortable with palliative care than euthanasia. The study stated:

> *"To reduce ... cognitive dissonance, they may choose to use opioids or sedatives because these drugs are not normally associated with euthanasia. Research has also shown that this kind of life ending practice might be more psychologically acceptable to physicians than bolus injection."* [75]

The researchers pointed out that since most of the unreported euthanasia deaths were done on people who appeared to be closer to death, the physician either felt under pressure to end the life of the patient or the physician felt that there was not enough time to go through the legal process.[76]

In response to the concern about time-frame or pressure, the authors of the study indicated that:

> *"The physician may ... prefer to use opioids or sedatives because these drugs are more readily available and there is less control over their distribution than with neuromuscular relaxants. By disguising euthanasia as pain alleviation, physicians can proceed with the euthanasia process without having to comply with the stringent, and in their perception time consuming, procedures of the euthanasia law."* [77]

To disguise euthanasia as palliative care relieves the physician of the requirement of reporting the death, but it also forgoes the safeguards that were intentionally built into the law.

Concerning the "safeguard" of the requirement to consult another physician, the study stated:

"Consultation occurred in almost all reported cases, whereas it occurred in only half of all unreported cases. This association was also found in the Netherlands,[78] where the most important reason for not consulting was that the physician did not intend to report the case. Physicians who intend to report a case seem to consult another physician and comply with the other requirements of the law, whereas physicians who do not intend to report a case appear to consult a physician only when they felt the need for the opinion of a colleague." [79]

The study concludes:

"As such legislation alone does not seem sufficient to reach the goal of transparency ("total" or a 100% transparency seems to be a rather utopian ideal) and to guarantee the careful practice of euthanasia." [80]

Conclusion:

This study shows that physicians are not reporting euthanasia deaths based on a few primary reasons. Often the physician does not consider the medical decision to constitute euthanasia. Other times, the physician never intended to report the death as euthanasia, and sometimes the physician will not report the euthanasia death because it is outside of the parameters of the law.

"... not one physician has faced prosecution for causing a death outside the parameters of the law."

Physicians who are not following the parameters of the law should be investigated by the Belgian Medical Association or prosecuted under the law. Smets et al., stated in the study "Legal Euthanasia in Belgium: Characteristics of All Reported Euthanasia Cases" that not one physician has faced prosecution for causing a death outside the parameters of the law.[81]

This study confirms that the reporting system in Belgium is insufficient to protect people from euthanasia. The reporting system is based on the physician voluntarily reporting the euthanasia death to the authorities. There is no procedure to ensure that all reports are sent in, and there is no assurance that the data that is sent into the authorities is accurate.

This study confirms that the reporting system in Belgium is insufficient to protect people from euthanasia.

When a physician or nurse decides to cause the death of a patient in a manner which is outside of the parameters of the law, the way to "get away with it" is to not report it as a euthanasia death.

This study shows that vulnerable people die by euthanasia in Belgium and these deaths are not being reported, making it an invisible crime.[82]

Any study or court decision that suggests that there is no indication that vulnerable groups are dying by euthanasia in jurisdictions where euthanasia and/or assisted suicide is legal is false. Data that is provided by the reporting procedures in the Netherlands, Belgium, Oregon and Washington State is limited. There are clear indications that vulnerable groups are at risk when euthanasia and/or assisted suicide are done outside of the law, and those cases are rarely reported.

This study shows that vulnerable people die by euthanasia in Belgium and these deaths are not being reported, making it an invisible crime.

Comparing Belgium to the Netherlands:

"Trends in end-of-life practices before and after the enactment of the euthanasia law in the Netherlands"

Lancet, July, 2012[83]

Similar to the previous cross-sectional studies that concerned the practice of euthanasia in the Netherlands during the years 2005 [84], 2001 [85], 1995 [86], and 1990 [87], the current meta-analysis compares 2010 to the previous studies and uncovers significant concerns related to euthanasia in the Netherlands.

It is important to compare the experience of legalized euthanasia in Belgium to that of the Netherlands because these countries both legalized euthanasia around a similar time and they both have similar euthanasia laws.

The study was done by mailing out 8,496 questionnaires to physicians to determine the frequency and their experience with euthanasia and assisted suicide. 6,263 of the questionnaires were returned and eligible for analysis (74% response rate).[88]

The increase in the rate of unreported euthanasia deaths in the Netherlands confirms the evidence documenting the practice in Belgium.

From 2005 to 2010 in the Netherlands, the percentage of unreported euthanasia deaths increased from 20% to 23%.[89] Even though the Netherlands has trained consultants to improve the practice of euthanasia, the number of unreported euthanasia deaths has increased.

The increase in the rate of unreported euthanasia deaths in the Netherlands confirms the statement by the authors of the study "Reporting of euthanasia in medical practice in Flanders, Belgium: cross sectional analysis of reported and unreported cases," who concluded that: "100% transparency seems to be a rather utopian ideal."[90]

The study determined that the demographic group for reported euthanasia deaths is: "mostly… younger people, cancer patients, and in general practice (in home) rather than in hospitals or nursing homes."[91] This is the same demographic group for reported euthanasia deaths in Belgium.[92] The study did not report the demographic group for the unreported euthanasia deaths. In Belgium, the demographic group for the unreported euthanasia deaths tended to be older.[93]

"100% transparency seems to be a rather utopian ideal."

The report found that there were approximately 310 assisted deaths without an explicit request in the Netherlands in 2010 [94], which was down from an estimated 550 assisted deaths without an explicit request in 2005.[95] In Belgium, the study "Physician-assisted deaths... " found that 32% of the euthanasia deaths in the Flanders region of Belgium were done without request or consent.[96]

The fact that the number of deaths without explicit request has dropped in the Netherlands appears optimistic, unless you are one of the 310 people.

The percentage of deaths by euthanasia and assisted suicide in the Netherlands increased from 1.8% of all deaths in 2005 to approximately 3.0% in 2010.[97] The actual number of euthanasia and assisted suicide deaths increased from 2,425 in 2005 to 4,050 in 2010.[98]

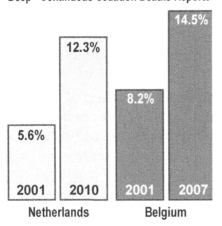

Deep - Continuous Sedation Deaths Reported

14.5%

12.3%

8.2%

5.6%

| 2001 | 2010 | 2001 | 2007 |
| Netherlands | | Belgium | |

At the same time, the number of deaths by deep-continuous sedation increased in the Netherlands from 8.2% of all deaths in 2005 to 12.3% of all deaths in 2010, representing a 50% increase. The rates of deep-continuous sedation are particularly concerning in both the Netherlands and Belgium. In Belgium, the article "Medical End-of-Life Practices under the Euthanasia Law in Belgium"[99] found that the rate of continuous or deep-continuous sedation in Belgium increased from 8.2% of all deaths in 2001 to 14.5% of all deaths in 2007.

Deep-continuous sedation is important because it can be abused. Physicians can sedate a person with the intention of palliation, normally referred to as palliative sedation, or the physician can sedate a patient with the intention of causing death, which is often referred to as terminal sedation. Research needs to be done, comparing the average doses of drug used to palliate symptoms as compared to the average doses of drugs used in the Netherlands, Belgium, or other jurisdictions, where the physician appears to intend to cause death.

Further data has recently become available. The 2011 Netherlands euthanasia statistics showed a continued increase in the rate of euthanasia. The number of euthanasia deaths in the Netherlands has increased by 18% in 2011, 19% in 2010 and 13% in 2009; and the number of euthanasia deaths in 2011 was more than double the number of euthanasia deaths in 2003.[100]

The Netherlands' euthanasia statistics suggest that the rate of euthanasia will increase on a constant basis until it reaches a point whereby euthanasia is considered medically acceptable and it becomes normalized.

The Netherlands' and Belgium's statistics indicate that not all doctors will follow the guidelines in the law. After 9 years of legal euthanasia in the Netherlands, 23% of all euthanasia deaths continue to be unreported,[101] and up to 47% of all euthanasia deaths in Belgium are unreported.[102]

Since the Netherlands did not publish the demographic data for the unreported euthanasia deaths, therefore, it is not possible at this time to show that vulnerable people are not adversely affected by the euthanasia law. It is also not possible to state that there is no evidence that vulnerable groups are adversely affected by euthanasia.

Comparing Belgium to the Netherlands

Legal Euthanasia in Belgium: Characteristics of All Reported Euthanasia Cases

Journal of Medical Care, February 2010[103]

This study examined every reported case of euthanasia in Belgium from September 22, 2002 to December 31, 2007. There were 1917 reported euthanasia deaths within that time-frame.[104]

In Belgium, euthanasia is defined as the intentional ending of life by a physician at the explicit request of a patient on condition that all the due care requirements prescribed in the law are satisfied.[105]

Euthanasia in Belgium is not limited to terminally ill people and it is not limited to physical suffering,[106] but rather suffering alone. Suffering is undefined, unclear and based on personal and not objective criteria. Suffering can only be determined by the person requesting euthanasia.[107]

The Belgian law requires a physician to obtain consent for euthanasia from a person who is terminally ill or suffering. A person requesting euthanasia who is not terminally ill must receive approval by a physician, a specialist and a psychiatrist.[108]

The study indicated that all of the data was collected from reports that are submitted by the physician who does the act of euthanasia (required by law). The study stated:

> *"Because of the anonymous nature of the notification procedure, it was impossible to contact the reporting physician for more in-depth information, or to match the reported cases to the corresponding death certificates."*[109]

The study acknowledged another weakness and stated:

> *"Death certificate data for Wallonia were not available for this period."*[110]

The study recognized that it is possible that unreported euthanasia deaths might have different characteristics than reported euthanasia deaths. However, the study only considered reported euthanasia deaths.[111]

The data from the study "Reporting of euthanasia in medical practice in Flanders Belgium: cross sectional analysis of reported and unreported cases" found that only 52.8% of all euthanasia deaths were reported. Therefore 47.2% of all euthanasia deaths are not reported.[112]

The research analysis overlooks the possibility that the data from the official reports may be inaccurate. The reports are received from the physician who carried out the act of euthanasia.[113] The report is, therefore, based on a self-reporting procedure. Doctors, like all others, are not likely to self-report abuse of the law, especially since it is possible that euthanasia deaths that are done outside of the legal practice may be investigated.[114] It is important to note that of the 1,917 reported euthanasia deaths, the Committee has never sent a reported case to the judicial authorities.[115, 116, 117]

The study found that the number of euthanasia deaths increased every year since euthanasia was legalized.[118] In 2010, there were 954 reported euthanasia deaths in Belgium.[119] Since Smets, Tinne, et al. "Reporting of euthanasia in medical practice in Flanders Belgium: cross sectional analysis of reported and unreported cases." found that only 52.8% of all euthanasia deaths were reported,[120] therefore the actual number of euthanasia deaths is much higher.

The study indicated that the demographic for the 1,917 reported euthanasia deaths was:

> *"men, younger patients, and cancer patients were significantly over-represented in euthanasia cases. Patients of 80 years or more were under-represented in all places of death among cancer and non-cancer patients."*[121]

The demographic for reported euthanasia deaths is similar to the demographic for reported euthanasia deaths in the Netherlands.[122]

The study stated that *"no evidence was found to support the fear that, once euthanasia is legalized, the lives of elderly patients would be more likely to be ended with assistance of a physician."*[123] We know from the other studies that this statement is false.

The study that found that 32% of all euthanasia deaths in the Flanders region of Belgium were done without explicit request[124] also indicated that the demographic group for unreported euthanasia deaths was: "patients who were 80 years of age or older (52.7%), those without cancer (67.5%) and those who died in hospital (67.1%)"[125]

The study concludes, *"Developments over time do not show any indication to support the slippery slope hypothesis."*[126] The data from this study does not allow the researchers to definitively back-up this statement. The study indicates that there is a high number of euthanasia deaths without explicit request but it does not analyze the data from this group.

The study is based on data that is limited to reported euthanasia deaths alone; and other studies found that the reported euthanasia deaths were usually done according to the rules of the law while the unreported euthanasia deaths often did not follow the rules of the law.[127]

... of the 1917 reported euthanasia deaths, the Committee has never sent a reported case to the judicial authorities.

If one were to base their conclusions on this study alone, one would think that all is well with the practice of euthanasia in Belgium. When considering studies that examined data from the large number of unreported euthanasia deaths and euthanasia deaths that were done by nurses and the euthanasia deaths done without explicit request, then we come to a very different conclusion.

Three Reports and One Court Decision That Have Drawn False or Misleading Conclusions

"Legal physician-assisted death in Oregon and the Netherlands: evidence concerning the impact on patients in "vulnerable" groups."[128] *the Journal of Medical Ethics (2007).*

The Royal Society of Canada Expert Panel: End-of-Life Decision Making Report[129] *seems to establish the foundation for the conclusions of subsequent reports in Canada.*

The Quebec government's Select Committee on Dying with Dignity Report[130] *concluded that euthanasia should be legalized in Quebec. It, too, influenced subsequent reports.*

Justice Lynn Smith, in Carter v. Canada (Attorney General)[131] *in British Columbia, decided that Canada's laws concerning euthanasia and assisted suicide are unconstitutional and over-broad.*

These studies appear to be written with the intent of forming the basis for legalizing euthanasia and assisted suicide in Canada and throughout the Western world.

The First Report

The first study, *"Legal physician-assisted death in Oregon and the Netherlands: evidence concerning the impact on patients in "vulnerable" groups,"* was completed under the leadership of Margaret Battin (University of Utah). This study looked at the official statistics from the Netherlands and Oregon, and other studies from both jurisdictions, and concluded that in the Netherlands and the State of Oregon, where euthanasia and/or assisted suicide have been legalized, that there is no proof that vulnerable people (other than people who are dying from AIDS) are more likely to die by euthanasia or assisted suicide. It concluded that the concept of a "slippery slope" is unfounded, and other than people with HIV, and no other vulnerable group is adversely effected by the legalization of euthanasia and assisted suicide.[132]

Battin came to her conclusion even though two studies from the Netherlands, which were published in 2004, indicated that euthanasia deaths that are reported tend to follow the guidelines but euthanasia deaths that are not reported tend not to comply with the guidelines.[133]

> *... euthanasia deaths that are not reported tend not to comply with the guidelines.*

The Second Report

The report of the *Royal Society of Canada Expert Panel: End-of-Life Decision Making*, November 2011,[134] concluded that Canada could "safely" legalize euthanasia and assisted suicide. This report also concluded that:

> *"Despite the fears of opponents, it is also clear that the much-feared slippery slope has not emerged following decriminalization, at least not in those jurisdictions for which evidence is available. Nor is there evidence to support the claim that permitting doctors to participate in bringing about the death of a patient has harmed the doctor/patient relationship. What has emerged is evidence that the law is capable of managing the decriminalization of assisted dying and that state policies on this issue can reassure citizens of their safety and well-being."*[135]

The Royal Society of Canada Report came to its conclusion even though it pointed out that there were approximately 550 deaths without request (Lawer) in 2005 in the Netherlands,[136] and deaths without request in Belgium represented 1.8% of all deaths in 2007; the report admitted that the proportion of involuntary euthanasia deaths were nearly identical to the percentage of voluntary euthanasia.[137]

> *... the proportion of involuntary euthanasia deaths was nearly identical to the percentage of voluntary euthanasia.*

The data concerning the high rate of euthanasia deaths without explicit request in Belgium was reported in the article *"Medical End-*

of-Life Practices under the Euthanasia Law in Belgium." This article was examined in *The Royal Society of Canada Report*. The article identified the concern related to unreported euthanasia deaths.

The question remains: Why did *The Royal Society of Canada Report* ignore Smets' analysis of the data provided in the study *"Reporting of euthanasia in medical practice in Flanders Belgium: cross sectional analysis of reported and unreported cases"*? Smets found, that unreported euthanasia deaths were more likely to be done to people who were older[138] representing a vulnerable patient group.

The Royal Society of Canada appointed an expert panel dominated by euthanasia lobby activists including:

- Jocelyn Downie, author of *Dying Justice: A Case for Decriminalizing Euthanasia and Assisted Suicide in Canada*[139]
- Sheila McLean, author of *Assisted Dying: Reflection on the Need for Law Reform*[140]
- Johannes J.M. van Delden, a long-time euthanasia promoter in the Netherlands, contributed to several reports on the practice of Euthanasia in the Netherlands.[141]

The acknowledgment at the beginning of *The Royal Society of Canada Report* recognizes several people for their help in the editing and production of the report including pro-euthanasia promoters:

- Dan Brock (Harvard)
- Helga Kuhse (Monash)
- Peter Singer (Princeton)
- Robert Young (La Trobe).[142]

It would appear that the Royal Society of Canada End-of-Life Decision Making panel was created to be one-sided in order to produce a one-sided report. The panel did not appear to be interested in open debate on the issues but they appear to be imposing a specific point of view upon society.[143] It also appears that the Royal Society of Canada Report drew false conclusions by limiting the scope of data.

... the panel did not appear to be interested in open debate on the issues.

But the problem did not end there. The Quebec commission founded its conclusions upon the *Royal Commision* report. The resulting Quebec National Assembly *Dying with Dignity* report reads like

The report reads like a "euthanasia manifesto."

a "Euthanasia Manifesto" according to an article written by Margaret Somerville in the Montreal Gazette, March 26.

The Third Report

The *Commission on Assisted Dying Report*[144] in the United Kingdom (also known as Lord Falconer's Report on Assisted Dying) was made up of pro-assisted suicide activists, was sponsored by Dignity in Dying (formerly known as the Voluntary Euthanasia Society) and received its funding from euthanasia campaigner, Terry Pratchett.[145]

The Commission on Assisted Dying Report concluded that the United Kingdom needed to legalize assisted suicide with safeguards.

The Legal Decision

In the *Carter v. Attorney General of Canada* decision, Justice Lynn Smith appeared to thoroughly examine the experience with euthanasia and assisted suicide in the jurisdictions where it is legal. With reference to Belgium, Smith analyzed most of the pertinent studies and came to a false conclusion.

In the *Carter* decision, Paragraph 575 responds to a question related to disability. She states that Professor Deliens declared that in the questionnaire, which was sent to physicians, that there was no question concerning disability; however, Deliens concludes that they could determine from the death certificates whether a person had a disability. He stated that they found no cases of disability.[146] This is an interesting conclusion considering the fact that many people have disabilities, especially later in life.

A questionable response by Justice Smith occurs when she looks at the question of euthanasia without request. She stated:

"Finally, I note that Professor Deliens was asked about the comment in the Chambaere et al. Population Study that 'the

use of life-ending drugs without explicit patient request occurred predominantly in hospital and among patients 80 years or older who were mostly in a coma or had dementia and fits the description of 'vulnerable' patient groups at risk of life ending without request.'"[147]

Smith responds to Professor Delien's evidence as follows:

"His responses to this line of questioning suggested that possibly he did not wish to admit that he had said that patients who are 80 years or older are vulnerable and at risk of LAWER. I take into account that Professor Deliens was ill, and was being cross-examined by videolink, in English (not his first language). Perhaps for those reasons, or perhaps because of a lack of impartiality, his responses in this one area did not seem wholly straightforward."[148]

The fact is that Deliens admitted that the Belgian research indicates that euthanasia deaths without request are more often done to a vulnerable patient group, as stated in the study *"Physician-assisted deaths under the euthanasia law in Belgium: a population-based survey."*[149] Why did Justice Smith then ignore his comment by providing some excuse that he was sick?

Why did Justice Smith then ignore Daliens' comments by providing some excuse that he was sick?

Three Reports and One Court Decision

Our Conclusions

The conclusions of *The Royal Society of Canada Expert Panel - End-of-Life Decision Making Report*,[150] and the *Quebec government's Select Committee on Dying with Dignity Report*[151] appear to be based on selective data from research that was limited to the official statistics from the reported euthanasia and/or assisted suicide deaths. These reports appear in their design to be intentionally oriented to establishing preconceived conclusions.

All of these reports, including the court decision by Justice Lynn Smith in *Carter v. Canada*, conclude that euthanasia in other jurisdictions, including Belgium, is occurring without threats to the lives of vulnerable groups. They further claim that there is no reasonable proof that a "slippery slope" exists.[152] This conclusion is false because it ignores all data that challenges this conclusion.

When examining the studies concerning the practice of euthanasia, the role of nurses and the reporting of euthanasia in Belgium, reasonable people must conclude that not all is well in Belgium.

The study *"Medical End-of-Life Practices under the Euthanasia Law in Belgium"*[153] found that euthanasia deaths without request or consent represent a different demographic group than those who die by euthanasia with consent.[154]

The study *"Physician-assisted deaths under the euthanasia law in Belgium: a population-based survey"*[155] found that 32% of the euthanasia deaths in the Flanders region of Belgium were done without explicit request.[156] This study determined that: *"the use of life-ending drugs without explicit patient request occurred predominantly in hospital and among patients 80 years or older who were mostly in coma or had dementia."*[157] This study found that there is a different demographic group for people who die by euthanasia without explicit request. The researchers stated that this "fits the description of "vulnerable" patient groups."[158] The same study also stated that:

> *"in the group without an explicit request, most of the patients had diseases other than cancer, which have less predictable end-of-life trajectories."*[159]

This is an important comment because it indicates that euthanasia is being done without an explicit request in order to control the timing of death.

The study *"The role of nurses in physician-assisted deaths in Belgium"*[160] proves that nurses are directly causing the death of their patients in Belgium (euthanasia) which is not legal in Belgium.

The study also determined that:

> *"factors significantly associated with the nurse administering the life-ending drugs were the absence of an explicit request from the patient, the patient being more than 80 years old and the nurse having had a recent experience with life-shortening end-of-life decisions."* [161]

Other factors associated with the nurse administering life-ending drugs were:

> *"... female nurses working in hospitals were six times and male nurses working in hospitals were 40 times more likely than their male and female counterparts working in other settings to administer the life-ending drugs."*[162]

The study *"Legal Euthanasia in Belgium: Characteristics of All Reported Euthanasia Cases,"*[163] which is referred to by *the Royal Society of Canada Report*, determined the characteristics of the 1,917 reported euthanasia deaths in Belgium. However, this study does not include the unreported euthanasia deaths in Belgium within its analysis. Therefore, the analysis by *The Royal Society of Canada Report* is inaccurate and misleading.

"... the 47.2% of euthanasia deaths that were not reported often did not follow the legal requirements.

The study *"Reporting of euthanasia in medical practice in Flanders Belgium: cross sectional analysis of reported and unreported cases"*[164] found that the 52.8% of euthanasia deaths that were reported were usually done in accordance with the legal requirements, but the 47.2% of the euthanasia deaths that were not reported often did not follow the legal requirements.[165] The same study also found that:

*"there was a significant relation between reporting of eutha-
nasia and the patient's age, with deaths of patients aged 80
years or older reported significantly less often than deaths
of younger patients."*[166]

Physicians indicated that some
of the reasons for not reporting
these death as euthanasia were:

**When the physician is con-
cerned that the euthanasia
death does not meet the legal
criteria, they do not report
the death as euthanasia.**

*"17.9% that reporting is too
much of an administrative
burden, 11.9% that the legal
due requirement had pos-
sibly not all been met, 8.7% that euthanasia is a private
matter between the physician and patient. A small proportion (2.3%) did not report the case because of possible legal
consequences."*[167]

When the physician is concerned that the euthanasia death does not
meet the legal criteria, they do not report the death as euthanasia.[168]

**... when physicians do not
intend to report the death as
euthanasia, they usually
do not consult
another physician, either.**

The same study determined
that when physicians do not intend to report the death as euthanasia, they usually do not consult
another physician either. The authors stated that:

*"This association was also
found in the Netherlands, where the most important reason
for not consulting was that the physician did not intend to
report the case."*[169]

The same study found that unreported euthanasia deaths were usually done by intentional opioid overdose. The study indicated that:

*"The physician may ... prefer to use opioids or sedatives be-
cause these drugs are more readily available and there is
less control over their distribution than with neuromuscular relaxants. By disguising euthanasia as pain alleviation,
physicians can proceed with the euthanasia process without
having to comply with the stringent, and in their perception
time consuming, procedures of the euthanasia law."*[170]

The authors of the study concluded that

"legislation alone does not seem sufficient to reach the goal of transparency ("total" or a 100% transparency seems to be a rather utopian ideal)."[171]

This statement directly contradicts Justice Lynn Smith's comments in her *Carter v. Canada* decision whereby she attempted to assure Canadians that euthanasia could be effectively legalized with safeguards.[172]

When analyzing the three Belgian studies concerning the practice of euthanasia, the role of nurses and the reporting of euthanasia in Belgium, one must conclude the following:

1. When a physician in Belgium reports a euthanasia death, as euthanasia, the physician usually follows the rules that are outlined by the law.[173]

2. When a physician does not report a euthanasia death, as euthanasia, the physician will often not follow the rules that are outlined by the law.[174]

3. When a euthanasia death is not reported, the patient is more likely to be over the age of 80, die in a hospital, and is often incompetent to consent to the act.[175] Euthanasia deaths that are done without explicit request are usually done to a person who is within the same demographic group. The same demographic is also over represented when a euthanasia death is done by a nurse. Therefore, euthanasia deaths that are done without explicit request, that are unreported, or that are done by nurses fit the same demographic group. This demographic group "fits the description of a "vulnerable" patient groups."[176]

4. Reasons for not reporting a euthanasia death, as euthanasia, include the following: to avoid the administrative burden, to avoid the fact that the legal due requirements are not met and to avoid possible legal consequences. Often the physician never intended to report the death as euthanasia.

5. Euthanasia deaths that are done by nurses in Belgium are not legal but occur on a regular basis; these deaths are usually done by order of a physician, but sometimes they were done without consulting the physician. These deaths are usually done by

intentional opioid overdose, even though sometimes they were done by neuromuscular relaxants, while 45% of the time they are done without explicit request. Nurses who had previously been involved with a euthanasia death and male nurses were far more likely to carry-out euthanasia in Belgium.

There are many areas of concern related to the practice of euthanasia in Belgium. Studies have also indicated that doctors in Belgium are not required to do euthanasia, but that they are required to refer a patient for euthanasia.[177] Similar to the Netherlands, Belgium considers euthanasia an option for people with dementia.[178] Belgium has also implemented rules related to euthanasia and organ donation.[179] In fact, the first person who died by euthanasia and organ donation was a person who was disabled and not terminally ill.[180]

The first person in Belgium who died of euthanasia followed by organ donation was disabled, and not terminally ill.

Depression and Euthanasia

Another concern related to euthanasia and assisted suicide that the Belgium studies did not investigate is the effect of depression on vulnerable persons. A study by a Dutch oncologist, *"Euthanasia and Depression: A Prospective Cohort Study Among Terminally Ill Cancer Patients,"* found that: "a request for euthanasia by patients with a depressed mood was 4.1 times higher than that of patients without a depressed mood."[181] The study concluded that:

> *"Our findings suggest that a depressed mood in the last months of life is associated with a higher risk for request for euthanasia."*[182]

A weakness in this study is that the authors did not include the number of people with a depressed mood who actually died by euthanasia.

A similar study, concerning depression which was done in the State of Oregon, entitled *"Prevalence of depression and anxiety in patients requesting physicians' aid in dying: cross sectional survey"* published in 2008 in the *British Medical Journal* found that of the 58 people who asked for assisted suicide and agreed to be part of the study, 15 were found to be depressed.[183] Of the 58 people in the study, 18 died by assisted suicide with 3 of them being among the group of depressed people.[184]

I do not know of a study concerning depression and euthanasia in Belgium, but it is likely that the results from the Netherlands and Oregon State would be similar in Belgium.

Increasing Numbers of Euthanasia Deaths

Another concern related to the implementation of euthanasia and assisted suicide laws is the growth over time in the number of deaths by euthanasia or assisted suicide. The study *"Legal Euthanasia in Belgium: Characteristics of All Reported Euthanasia Cases"* states that from September 22, 2002 to December 31, 2007, 1,917 euthanasia deaths were reported in Belgium.[185] The study also indicates that the number of euthanasia deaths increased every year since euthanasia was legalized.[186] In 2010, there were 954 reported euthanasia deaths in Belgium.[187]

In the Netherlands, the number of reported euthanasia deaths has grown significantly in the past few years. The statistics concerning the

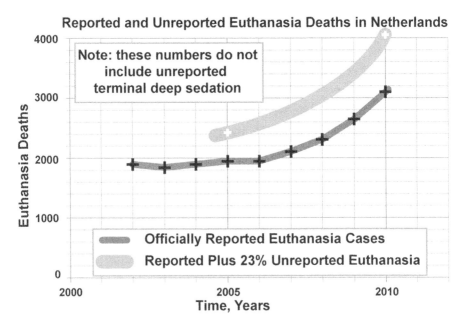

Reported and Unreported Euthanasia Deaths in Netherlands

Note: these numbers do not include unreported terminal deep sedation

Euthanasia Deaths

■■■ Officially Reported Euthanasia Cases

Reported Plus 23% Unreported Euthanasia

Time, Years

number of reported euthanasia deaths in the Netherlands are as follows: 2006 – 1,923 deaths, 2007 – 2,120 deaths, 2008 – 2,331 deaths, 2009 – 2,636 deaths, 2010 – 3,136 deaths, and 2011 – 3,695 deaths.[188] These statistics do not include the assisted suicide deaths or the unreported euthanasia deaths that in 2010 were estimated to be 23% of all euthanasia deaths in the Netherlands.[189]

In Belgium, not one physician has faced prosecution for causing a death (euthanasia) outside the parameters of the law,[190] even though there is clear proof of each of the following: nurses are lethally injecting people, which is outside of the law;[191] euthanasia deaths are occurring without explicit request which is outside of the law;[192] as high as 47% of euthanasia cases are not being reported, which is outside of the law;[193] and a large number of the unreported euthanasia deaths occur without the physician ever intending to report the death as euthanasia.[194]

Those who support euthanasia and assisted suicide will often refer to the reporting procedure as a safeguard to ensure that the law is not abused. The reporting procedure for assisted suicide in the states of Oregon and Washington, where assisted suicide is legal, is very similar to the reporting procedure for euthanasia in Belgium and the Netherlands. All of these jurisdictions require the physician to report the euthanasia or assisted suicide death after the person has died; and the report is sent into the authorities by the doctor who caused the death, in the case of euthanasia, or by the doctor who wrote the prescription for the lethal dose, in the case of assisted suicide.

The reporting procedure in the Netherlands, Belgium, Oregon State and Washington State do not protect people from abuse because of the following:

1. The person has died already once the report is sent into the authorities. No protection is provided from abuse by an after-the-death reporting procedure. You cannot reverse the act.

2. The study in Belgium, that stated that 32% of all euthanasia deaths were unreported, found that when a physician did not follow the guidelines in the law, or when the death was outside the parameters of the law, the physician usually did not report the death as a euthanasia death.[195] It must be noted that the

2010 study from the Netherlands found that 23% of all euthanasia deaths went unreported.[196]

3. If an abuse of the law occurs and the physician reports the euthanasia death, will the doctor self-report abuse?

When considering an issue of life and death, can a nation consider any level of intentional killings as acceptable? When considering that euthanasia concerns people who are die by lethal injection and assisted suicide occurs by intentional lethal overdose, can society ensure that every citizen will be safe?

To state that there are few, if any, concerns related to the practice of euthanasia in Belgium is clearly false, and to state that there are no indications of a "slippery slope" effect in Belgium is false and misleading.

The fact is that there has been a clear growth and an increased promotion of euthanasia and assisted suicide. Euthanasia and assisted suicide are becoming accepted for more and more reasons, and there are few effective controls to protect vulnerable people from it.

Society needs to ensure that every person is cared for and treated with dignity and it must limit its actions to non-lethal means to alleviate suffering.

By exposing vulnerable people to euthanasia and assisted suicide the life that will be taken could include yours, your mother's, or that of someone who needs to be cared for and not to be killed.

Bibliography

Registratiedocument euthanasie. Belgian registration form euthanasia [in Dutch and French]. (2002).

Wet betreffende euthanasie 28 Mei, 2002. Law concerning euthanasia May 28, 2002. (2002, Juni 22). Belgisch Staatsblad 22 Juni, 2002. Belgium official collection of the laws June 22, 2002 [in Dutch].

Battin, M. P., van der Heide, A., Ganzini, L., van der Wal, G., & Onwuteaka, B. D. (October 2007, October). Legal physician-assisted death in Oregon and the Netherlands: evidence concerning the impact on patients in "vulnerable" groups. Journal of Medical Ethics, 591-597.

Bilsen, J., Cohen, J., Chambaere, K., Pousset, G., Onwuteaka-Philipsen, B. D., Mortier, F., et al. (2009, September 10). Medical End-of-Life Practices under the Euthanasia Law in Belgium. New England Journal of Medicine, 1119-1121.

Cellarius, D. V. (2010, June 23). Assisted Death Without Consent? A Response to 'The role of nurses in physician-assisted deaths in Belgium,' by Dr. Victor Cellarius, Tammy Latner Centre for Palliative Care, Mount Sinai Hospital Toronto. Canadian Medical Association Journal.

Chambaere, K., Bilsen, J., Cohen, J., Onwuteaka-Philipsen, B. D., Mortier, F., & Deliens, L. (2010, June 15). Physician-assisted deaths under the euthanasia law in Belgium: a population-based survey. Canadian Medical Association Journal, 895-901.

Commission on Assisted Dying. (January 5, 2012). The Commission on Assisted Dying Report. London: Secretariat for the Commission on Assisted Dying:

Detry, O., Laureys, S., Faymondville, M.-E., De Roover, A., Squifflet, J.-P., Lamy, M., et al. (2008). Organ donation after physician-assisted death. European Society for Organ Transplantation, 915.

Downie, J. (2004). Dying Justice: A case for decriminalizing euthanasia and assisted suicide in Canada. Toronto: University of Toronto.

Ganzini, L., Goy, E. R., & Dobscha, S. K. (2008). Prevalence of depression and anxiety in patients requesting physicians' aid in dying: cross sectional survey. British Medical Journal, 1682-1687.

Inghelbrecht, E. (2010, June 30). Response to Victor Cellarius, ie: The role of nurses in physician-assisted deaths in Belgium, by Els Inghelbrecht, End-of-Life Care Research Group, Vrije Universiteit Brussel. Canadian

Medical Association Journal.

Inghelbrecht, E., Bilsen, J., Mortier, F., & Deliens, L. (2009, September). Attitudes of nurses toward euthanasia and towards their role in euthanasia: a nationwide study in Flanders Belgium. International Journal of Nursing Studies, 1209-1218.

Inghelbrecht, E., Bilsen, J., Mortier, F., & Deliens, L. (2010, June 15). The role of nurses in physician-assisted deaths in Belgium. Canadian Medical Association Journal, 905-910.

Jansen-van der Weide, M., Onwuteaka-Philipsen, B., & van der Wal, G. (2004, September). Implementation of the project 'Support and Consultation on Euthanasia in the Netherlands' (SCEN). Health Policy, 365-373.

McLean, S. (2007). Assisted Dying: Reflections on the Need for Law Reform. Routledge-Cavendish.

Nys, H. (2003). A presentation of the Belgian Act on euthanasia against the background of Dutch euthanasia law. Eur J Health Law, 10:239-255.

Onwuteaka-Philipsen, B. D., Brinkman-Stoppelenburg, A., Penning, C., de Jong-Krul, G. J., van Delden, J. J., & van der Heide, A. (2012, July 11). Trends in end-of-life practices before and after the enactment of the euthanasia law in the Netherlands from 1990 to 2010: a repeated cross-sectional survey. The Lancet.

Onwuteaka-Philipsen, B., van der Heide, A., & Koper, D. (2003). Euthanasia and other end-of-life decisions in the Netherlands in 1990, 1995, and 2001. Lancet, 362, 395-99.

Pollard, B. (2001). Can euthanasia be safely legalized? Palliat Med, 15:61-65.

Quebec, G. o. (2012, March 22). Select Committee on Dying with Dignity Report. Retrieved from Assemblée Nationale Québec: http://www.assnat. qc.ca/fr/actualites-salle-presse/nouvelle/Actualite-25939.html

Schadenberg, A. (2011, August). Euthanasia Is Out-of-Control in Belgium. Retrieved from AlexSchadenberg.blogspot.ca: http://alexschadenberg. blogspot.ca/2011/08/euthanasia-is-out-of-control-in-belgium.html

Schadenberg, A. (2011, November 14). Royal Society of Canada - one sided report - to be released tomorrow.

Schadenberg, A. (2012, September 25). Euthanasia is out-of-control in the Netherlands - New Dutch Statistics.

Schadenberg, A. (2012, January 5). One-sided assisted suicide report released in the UK.

Schadenberg, A. (n.d.). AlexSchadenberg.blogspot.ca. Retrieved from Alex-Schadenberg.blogspot.ca: http://www.alexschadenberg.blogspot.ca

Schuklenk, U., van Delden, J. J., Downie, J., McLean, S., Upshur, R., & Weinstock, D. (November 2011). The Royal Society of Canada Expert Panel: End-of-Life Decision Making Report. Ottawa: The Royal Society of Canada.

Federale controle-en evaluatiecommissie voor euthanasie. Eerste verslag aan de wetgevende kamers 22 September 2002-31 December 2003, 2004. Federal control and evaluation committee on euthanasia. Second report to Parliament [in Dutch and French]. (September 22, 2002-December 31, 2003 [Published 2004]).

Smets, T., Bilsen, J., Cohen, J., Rurup, M. L., & Deliens, L. (2010, February). Legal Euthanasia in Belgium: Characteristics of All Reported Euthanasia Cases. Journal of Medical Care, 187-192.

Smets, T., Bilsen, J., Cohen, J., Rurup, M. L., Mortier, F., & Deliens, L. (2010, October 5). Reporting of euthanasia in medical practice in Flanders Belgium: cross sectional analysis of reported and unreported cases. British Medical Journal, 5174-5182.

Smith, J. L. (2012, June 15). Carter v. Canada (Attorney General), 2012 BCSC 886. Retrieved from British Columbia Civil Liberties Association: http://bccla.org/wp-content/uploads/2012/06/Carter-v-Canada-AG-2012-BCSC-886.pdf

Statistiek, C. B. (2012, July 11). Deaths by medical end-of-life decision; age, cause of death. Statistics Netherlands.

The Belgium Association of General Practitioners. (2003). Policy Statement on End of Life Decisions and Euthanasia. Brussels.

van der Heide, A., Onwuteaka-Philipsen, B., & Rurup, M. (2007). End-of-life practices in the Netherlands under the Euthanasia Act. New England Journal of Medicine, 356, 1957-65.

van der Lee, M. L., van der Bom, J. G., Swarte, N. B., Heintz, A. M., de Graeff, A., & van den Bout, J. (2005). Euthanasia and Depression: A Prospective Cohort Study Among Terminally Ill Cancer Patients. Journal of Clinical Oncology, 23, 6607-6612.

Van Der Maas, P., Van Delden, J., Pijnenborg, L., & Looman, C. (1991). Euthanasia and other medical decisions concerning the end of life. Lancet, 338, 669-74.

van der Wal, G., van der Mass, P., & Haverkate, I. (1996). Euthanasia and other end-of-life decisions in the Netherlands 1990-1995. New England Journal of Medicine, 335, 1699-1705.

Ysebaert, D., Van Beeumen, G., De Greef, K., Squifflet, J., Detry, O., De Roover, A., et al. (2009). Organ Procurement After Euthanasia: Belgian Experience. Transplantation Proceedings(41), 585–586.

Endnotes

1 AlexSchadenberg.blogspot.ca. n.d. Blogs: See Lord Falconer, Margaret Battin or Royal Society of Canada. <http://www.alexschadenberg.blogspot.ca>.

2 Bilsen, Johan, et al. "Medical End-of-Life Practices under the Euthanasia Law in Belgium." New England Journal of Medicine (2009): 1119-1121. Journal Article. <http://www.nejm.org/doi/pdf/10.1056/NEJMc0904292>.

3 Bilsen, Johan, et al. "Medical End-of-Life Practices under the Euthanasia Law in Belgium.", 1119.

4 Chambaere, Kenneth, et al. "Physician-assisted deaths under the euthanasia law in Belgium: a population-based survey." Canadian Medical Association Journal (2010): 895.

5 Bilsen, Johan, et al., 1119.

6 Bilsen, Johan, et al., 1120.

7 Bilsen, Johan, et al., 1120.

8 Bilsen, Johan, et al., 1119.

9 Onwuteaka-Philipsen, Bregje D, et al. "Trends in end-of-life practices before and after the enactment of the euthanasia law in the Netherlands from 1990 to 2010: a repeated cross-sectional survey." The Lancet (2012): 908 - 915. Journal Article. <http://press.thelancet.com/netherlands_euthanasia.pdf>.

10 Onwuteaka-Philipsen, Bregje D, et al.

11 Bilsen, Johan, et al. "Medical End-of-Life Practices under the Euthanasia Law in Belgium.", 1119

12 Bilsen, Johan, et al., 1119.

13 Bilsen, Johan, et al., 1119.

14 Chambaere, Kenneth, et al. "Physician-assisted deaths under the euthanasia law in Belgium: a population-based survey."

15 Chambaere, Kenneth, et al., 895

16 Chambaere, Kenneth, et al., 895.

17 Chambaere, Kenneth, et al., 896.

18 Chambaere, Kenneth, et al. 896.

19 Chambaere, Kenneth, et al. 896.

20 Chambaere, Kenneth, et al. 897.

21 Chambaere, Kenneth, et al. 897.

22 Chambaere, Kenneth, et al. 897.

23 Chambaere, Kenneth, et al. 897.

24 Chambaere, Kenneth, et al. 897.

25 Chambaere, Kenneth, et al. 899.

26 Chambaere, Kenneth, et al., 899.

27 Smets, T., et al. "Legal Euthanasia in Belgium: Characteristics of All Reported Eutha-
    nasia Cases."

28 Chambaere, Kenneth, et al. "Physician-assisted deaths under the euthanasia law in
    Belgium: a population-based survey.", 896.

29 Schuklenk, Udo, et al. (November 2011). The Royal Society of Canada Expert Panel:
    End-of-Life Decision Making Report. Ottawa: The Royal Society of Canada., 90.

30 Smets, Tinne, et al. "Reporting of euthanasia in medical practice in Flanders Bel-
    gium: cross sectional analysis of reported and unreported cases." British Medical
    Journal (2010): 5178. Journal Article.

31 Chambaere, Kenneth, et al. "Physician-assisted deaths under the euthanasia law in
    Belgium: a population-based survey.", 899.

32 Inghelbrecht, Els, et al. "The role of nurses in physician-assisted deaths in Belgium."
    Canadian Medical Association Journal (2010): 905-910.

33 Inghelbrecht, Els, et al., 905.

34 Inghelbrecht, Els, et al., 906.

35 Inghelbrecht, Els, et al., 906.

36 Inghelbrecht, Els, et al., 906.

37 Inghelbrecht, Els, et al., 906.

38 Inghelbrecht, Els, et al., 905.

39 Inghelbrecht, Els, et al., 909.

40 Inghelbrecht, Els, et al., 906 – 907.

41 Inghelbrecht, Els, et al., 907.

42 Chambaere, Kenneth, et al. "Physician-assisted deaths under the euthanasia law in
    Belgium: a population-based survey."

43 Chambaere, Kenneth, et al.,896.

44 Inghelbrecht, Els, et al. "The role of nuses in physician-assisted deaths in Belgium."
    907.

45 Inghelbrecht, Els, et al., 907.

46 Inghelbrecht, Els, et al., 907.

47 Inghelbrecht, Els, et al., 907.

48 Inghelbrecht, Els, et al., 907.

49 Inghelbrecht, Els, et al., 907.

50 Inghelbrecht, Els, et al. "Attitudes of nurses toward euthanasia and towards their role
    in euthanasia: a nationwide study in Flanders Belgium." International Journal of
    Nursing Studies (2009): 1209-1218.

51 Inghelbrecht, Els, et al., "The role of nurses in physician-assisted deaths in Belgium."
    909.

52 Inghelbrecht, Els, et al., 910.

53 Inghelbrecht, Els, et al., 910.

54 Inghelbrecht, Els, et al., 909.

55 Smets, T., et al. "Legal Euthanasia in Belgium: Characteristics of All Reported Euthanasia Cases."

56 Inghelbrecht, Els, et al. "The role of nurses in physician-assisted deaths in Belgium.", 909.

57 Inghelbrecht, Els, et al. "The role of nurses in physician-assisted deaths in Belgium."

58 Canadian Medical Association Journal (2010) online edition: <http://www.cmaj.ca/content/182/9/905.full/reply#cmaj_el_532553>.

59 Inghelbrecht, Els, et al. "The role of nurses in physician-assisted deaths in Belgium."

60 Cellarius, Dr. Victor. "Assisted Death Without Consent? A Response to 'The role of nurses in physician-assisted deaths in Belgium,' Dr. Victor Cellarius, Tammy Latner Centre for Palliative Care, Mount Sinai Hospital Toronto." Canadian Medical Association Journal (2010). Response. <http://www.cmaj.ca/content/182/9/905.full/reply#cmaj_el_532553>.

61 Cellarius, Dr. Victor. "Assisted Death Without Consent? A Response to 'The role of nurses in physician-assisted deaths in Belgium,'

62 Inghelbrecht, Els. "Response to Victor Cellarius, ie: The role of nurses in physician-assisted deaths in Belgium, Els Inghelbrecht, End-of-Life Care4 Research Group, Vrije Universiteit Brussel."

63 Inghelbrecht, Els. "Response to Victor Cellarius, ie: The role of nurses in physician-assisted deaths in Belgium."

64 Smets, Tinne, et al. "Reporting of euthanasia in medical practice in Flanders Belgium: cross sectional analysis of reported and unreported cases."

65 Smets, Tinne, et al., 5174.

66 Smets, Tinne, et al., 5174.

67 Smets, Tinne, et al., 5174.

68 Smets, Tinne, et al., 5177 – 5178.

69 Chambaere, Kenneth, et al. "Physician-assisted deaths under the euthanasia law in Belgium: a population-based survey."

70 Smets, Tinne, et al. "Reporting of euthanasia in medical practice in Flanders Belgium: cross sectional analysis of reported and unreported cases.", 5178.

71 Smets, Tinne, et al., 5178.

72 Smets, Tinne, et al., 5181.

73 Smets, Tinne, et al., 5181.

74 Smets, Tinne, et al., 5181 - 5182.

75 Smets, Tinne, et al., 5182

76 Smets, Tinne, et al., 5183

77 Smets, Tinne, et al., 5183

78 Jansen-van der Weide, MC, BD Onwuteaka-Philipsen and G. van der Wal. "Implementation of the project 'Support and Consultation on Euthanasia in the Nether-

lands' (SCEN)."

79 Smets, Tinne, et al. "Reporting of euthanasia in medical practice in Flanders Belgium: cross sectional analysis of reported and unreported cases.", 5183.

80 Smets, Tinne, et al., 5183

81 Smets, T., et al. "Legal Euthanasia in Belgium: Characteristics of All Reported Euthanasia Cases.", 191.

82 Smets, Tinne, et al. "Reporting of euthanasia in medical practice in Flanders Belgium: cross sectional analysis of reported and unreported cases.", 5178.

83 Onwuteaka-Philipsen, Bregje D, et al. "Trends in end-of-life practices before and after the enactment of the euthanasia law in the Netherlands from 1990 to 2010: a repeated cross-sectional survey."

84 van der Heide A, Onwuteaka-Philipsen BC, Rurup ML, et al. End-of-life practices in the Netherlands under the Euthanasia Act, N. Eng J Med 2007; 356: 1957-65.

85 Onwuteaka-Philipsen, BD., A. van der Heide and D. Koper. "Euthanasia and other end-of-life decisions in the Netherlands in 1990, 1995, and 2001." Lancet 362 (2003): 395-99.

86 van der Wal, G., PJ. van der Mass and I. Haverkate. "Euthanasia and other end-of-life decisions in the Netherlands 1990-1995." New England Journal of Medicine 335 (1996): 1699-1705.

87 Van Der Maas, PJ, et al. "Euthanasia and other medical decisions concerning the end of life." Lancet 338 (1991): 669-74.

88 Onwuteaka-Philipsen, Bregje D, et al. "Trends in end-of-life practices before and after the enactment of the euthanasia law in the Netherlands from 1990 to 2010: a repeated cross-sectional survey.", 911.

89 Onwuteaka-Philipsen, Bregje D, et al., 913.

90 Smets, Tinne, et al., "Reporting of euthanasia in medical practice in Flanders Belgium: cross sectional analysis of reported and unreported cases.", 5183.

91 Onwuteaka-Philipsen, Bregje D, et al., 913.

92 Smets, T., et al. "Legal Euthanasia in Belgium: Characteristics of All Reported Euthanasia Cases."

93 Smets, Tinne, et al. "Reporting of euthanasia in medical practice in Flanders Belgium: cross sectional analysis of reported and unreported cases.", 5178

94 Statistiek, Central Bureau voor de. "Deaths by medical end-of-life decision; age, cause of death." Statistics Netherlands (2012). report. <http://statline.cbs.nl/StatWeb/publication/?VW=T&DM=SLen&PA=81655ENG&LA=en>

95 van der Heide A, Onwuteaka-Philipsen BC, Rurup ML, et al. 1961.

96 Smets, Tinne, et al. "Reporting of euthanasia in medical practice in Flanders Belgium: cross sectional analysis of reported and unreported cases.", 5174.

97 Onwuteaka-Philipsen, Bregje D, et al. "Trends in end-of-life practices before and after the enactment of the euthanasia law in the Netherlands from 1990 to 2010: a repeated cross-sectional survey.", 910.

98 Onwuteaka-Philipsen, Bregje D, et al., 913.

99 Bilsen, Johan, et al. "Medical End-of-Life Practices under the Euthanasia Law in Belgium." New England Journal of Medicine (2009): 1119-1121.

100 Schadenberg, Alex., "Euthanasia is out-of-control in the Netherlands - New Dutch Statistics." (2012). blog.

101 Onwuteaka-Philipsen, Bregje D, et al., 913.

102 Smets, Tinne, et al. "Reporting of euthanasia in medical practice in Flanders Belgium: cross sectional analysis of reported and unreported cases.", 5174.

103 Smets, T., et al. "Legal Euthanasia in Belgium: Characteristics of All Reported Euthanasia Cases." Journal of Medical Care (2010): 187-192.

104 Smets, T., et al., 187.

105 "Wet betreffende euthanasie 28 Mei, 2002. Law concerning euthanasia May 28, 2002." Belgisch Staatsblad 22 Juni, 2002. Belgium official collection of the laws June 22, 2002 [in Dutch] (2002). Law.

106 "Federale controle-en evaluatiecommissie voor euthanasie. Eerste verslag aan de wetgevende kamers 22 September 2002-31 December 2003, 2004. Federal control and evaluation committee on euthanasia. Second report to Parliament [in Dutch and French]." September 22, 2002-December 31, 2003 [Published 2004]. Report. <http://www.senate.be/www/?Mlval=/index_enate&MENUID=12420&LANG=fr>.

107 Nys, H. "A presentation of the Belgian Act on euthanasia against the background of Dutch euthanasia law." Eur J Health Law (2003): 10:239-255.

108 "Wet betreffende euthanasie 28 Mei, 2002. Law concerning euthanasia May 28, 2002."

109 Smets, T., et al. "Legal Euthanasia in Belgium: Characteristics of All Reported Euthanasia Cases.", 188.

110 Smets, T., et al., 188.

111 Smets, T., et al., 191.

112 Smets, Tinne, et al. "Reporting of euthanasia in medical practice in Flanders Belgium: cross sectional analysis of reported and unreported cases.", 5174.

113 Smets, T., et al. "Legal Euthanasia in Belgium: Characteristics of All Reported Euthanasia Cases.", 187.

114 Smets, Tinne, et al. "Reporting of euthanasia in medical practice in Flanders Belgium: cross sectional analysis of reported and unreported cases.", 5177 – 5178.

115 Federale controle-en evaluatiecommissie voor euthanasie. Eerste verslag aan de wetgevende kamers 22 September 2002-31 December 2003, 2004. Federal control and evaluation committee on euthanasia. Second report to Parliament [in Dutch and French]. September 22, 2002-December 31, 2003 [Published 2004].

116 Pollard, BJ. "Can euthanasia be safely legalized?" Palliat Med (2001): 15:61-65.

117 "Registratiedocument euthanasie. Belgian registration form euthanasia [in Dutch and French]." (2002). Registration Form.

118 Smets, T., et al. "Legal Euthanasia in Belgium: Characteristics of All Reported Euthanasia Cases.", 188.

119 Schadenberg, Alex. Euthanasia Is Out-of-Control in Belgium. August 2011. Blog.

120 Smets, Tinne, et al. "Reporting of euthanasia in medical practice in Flanders Belgium: cross sectional analysis of reported and unreported cases.", 5174.

121 Smets, T., et al. "Legal Euthanasia in Belgium: Characteristics of All Reported Euthanasia Cases.", 187.

122 Onwuteaka-Philipsen, Bregje D, et al., 913.

123 Smets, T., et al. "Legal Euthanasia in Belgium: Characteristics of All Reported Euthanasia Cases.", 191.

124 Chambaere, Kenneth, et al. "Physician-assisted deaths under the euthanasia law in Belgium: a population-based survey.", 895.

125 Chambaere, Kenneth, et al., 896.

126 Smets, T., et al., "Legal Euthanasia in Belgium: Characteristics of All Reported Euthanasia Cases.", 192.

127 Smets, Tinne, et al. "Reporting of euthanasia in medical practice in Flanders Belgium: cross sectional analysis of reported and unreported cases.", 5174

128 Battin, Margaret P, et al. "Legal physician-assisted death in Oregon and the Netherlands: evidence concerning the impact on patients in "vulnerable" groups." Journal of Medical Ethics (October 2007): 591-597.

129 Schuklenk, Udo, et al. The Royal Society of Canada Expert Panel: End-of-Life Decision Making Report.

130 Government, Quebec. Select Committee on Dying with Dignity Report. 22 March 2012. Assemblée Nationale Québec.

131 Smith, Justice Lynn. "Carter v. Canada (Attorney General), 2012 BCSC 886." 15 June 2012.

132 Battin, Margaret P, et al. "Legal physician-assisted death in Oregon and the Netherlands: evidence concerning the impact on patients in "vulnerable" groups."

133 Smets, Tinne, et al. "Reporting of euthanasia in medical practice in Flanders Belgium: cross sectional analysis of reported and unreported cases.", 5181.

134 Schuklenk, Udo, et al. The Royal Society of Canada Expert Panel: End-of-Life Decision Making Report. Final Report. Ottawa: The Royal Society of Canada, November 2011.

135 Schuklenk, Udo, et al., 90.

136 Schuklenk, Udo, et al., 85.

137 Schuklenk, Udo, et al., 86.

138 Smets, Tinne, et al. "Reporting of euthanasia in medical practice in Flanders Belgium: cross sectional analysis of reported and unreported cases.", 5178.

139 Downie, J. (2004). Dying Justice: A case for decriminalizing euthanasia and assisted suicide in Canada. Toronto: University of Toronto.

140 McLean, S. (2007). Assisted Dying: Reflections on the Need for Law Reform. Routledge-Cavendish.

141 Schadenberg, Alex. "Royal Society of Canada - one sided report - to be released tomorrow." (2011). blog.

142 Schuklenk, Udo, et al., 1.

143 Schadenberg, Alex. "Royal Society of Canada - one sided report - to be released tomorrow." (2011). blog.

144 The Commission on Assisted Dying Report. Final Report. Commission on Assisted Dying. London: Secretariat for the Commission on Assisted Dying: Demos, January 5, 2012.

145 Schadenberg, Alex. "One-sided assisted suicide report released in the UK." (2012). blog.

146 Smith, Justice Lynn. "Carter v. Canada (Attorney General), 2012 BCSC 886.", 575.

147 Smith, Justice Lynn. "Carter v. Canada (Attorney General), 2012 BCSC 886.", 576.

148 Smith, Justice Lynn. "Carter v. Canada (Attorney General), 2012 BCSC 886.", 577.

149 Chambaere, Kenneth, et al. "Physician-assisted deaths under the euthanasia law in Belgium: a population-based survey.", 899.

150 Schuklenk, Udo, et al. The Royal Society of Canada Expert Panel: End-of-Life Decision Making Report.

151 Quebec, Government of. "Select Committee on Dying with Dignity Report."

152 Schuklenk, Udo, et al., The Royal Society of Canada Expert Panel: End-of-Life Decision Making Report. 90.

153 Bilsen, Johan, et al. "Medical End-of-Life Practices under the Euthanasia Law in Belgium."

154 Bilsen, Johan, et al. 1120.

155 Chambaere, Kenneth, et al. "Physician-assisted deaths under the euthanasia law in Belgium: a population-based survey."

156 Chambaere, Kenneth, et al. 896.

157 Chambaere, Kenneth, et al. 898.

158 Chambaere, Kenneth, et al. 899.

159 Chambaere, Kenneth, et al. 899.

160 Inghelbrecht, Els, et al. "The role of nurses in physician-assisted deaths in Belgium."

161 Inghelbrecht, Els, et al., 907.

162 Inghelbrecht, Els, et al., 907.

163 Smets, T., et al. "Legal Euthanasia in Belgium: Characteristics of All Reported Euthanasia Cases."

164 Smets, Tinne, et al. "Reporting of euthanasia in medical practice in Flanders Belgium: cross sectional analysis of reported and unreported cases."

165 Smets, Tinne, et al., 5174.

166 Smets, Tinne, et al., 5178.

167 Smets, Tinne, et al., 5178.

168 Smets, Tinne, et al., 5178.

169 Smets, Tinne, et al., 5181.

170 Smets, Tinne, et al., 5180.

171 Smets, Tinne, et al., 5181.

172 Smith, Justice Lynn. "Carter v. Canada (Attorney General), 2012 BCSC 886." 15 June 2012

173 Smets, Tinne, et al. "Reporting of euthanasia in medical practice in Flanders Belgium: cross sectional analysis of reported and unreported cases.", 5174.

174 Inghelbrecht, Els, et al. "The role of nurses in physician-assisted deaths in Belgium.", 909.

175 Smets, Tinne, et al. "Reporting of euthanasia in medical practice in Flanders Belgium: cross sectional analysis of reported and unreported cases.", 5178.

176 Chambaere, Kenneth, et al. "Physician-assisted deaths under the euthanasia law in Belgium: a population-based survey.", 899.

177 The Belgium Association of General Practitioners. (2003). Policy Statement on End of Life Decisions and Euthanasia. Brussels.

178 Schadenberg, A. (2011, August). Euthanasia Is Out-of-Control in Belgium. Blog.

179 Ysebaert, D., et al. "Organ Procurement After Euthanasia: Belgian Experience." Transplantation Proceedings 41 (2009): 585–586.

180 Detry, O., Laureys, S., Faymondville, M.-E., De Roover, A., Squifflet, J.-P., Lamy, M., et al. (2008). Organ donation after physician-assisted death. European Society for Organ Transplantation , 915.

181 van der Lee, M. L., van der Bom, J. G., Swarte, N. B., Heintz, A. M., de Graeff, A., & van den Bout, J. (2005). Euthanasia and Depression: A Prospective Cohort Study Among Terminally Ill Cancer Patients., 6609.

182 van der Lee, M. L., et al., 6611.

183 Ganzini, L., Goy, E. R., & Dobscha, S. K. (2008). Prevalence of depression and anxiety in patients requesting physicians' aid in dying: cross sectional survey., 1682.

184 Ganzini, L., et al., 1682.

185 Smets, T., et al. "Legal Euthanasia in Belgium: Characteristics of All Reported Euthanasia Cases."

186 Smets, T., et al., 188.

187 Schadenberg, Alex. Euthanasia Is Out-of-Control in Belgium. August 2011. Blog.

188 Schadenberg, A. (2012, September 25). Euthanasia is out-of-control in the Netherlands.

189 Onwuteaka-Philipsen, Bregje D, et al. "Trends in end-of-life practices before and after the enactment of the euthanasia law in the Netherlands from 1990 to 2010: a repeated cross-sectional survey.", 913.

190 Smets, T., et al. "Legal Euthanasia in Belgium: Characteristics of All Reported Euthanasia Cases.", 191.

191 Inghelbrecht, Els, et al. "The role of nurses in physician-assisted deaths in Belgium."

192 Chambaere, Kenneth, et al. "Physician-assisted deaths under the euthanasia law in Belgium: a population-based survey."

193 Smets, Tinne, et al. "Reporting of euthanasia in medical practice in Flanders Belgium: cross sectional analysis of reported and unreported cases."

194 Smets, Tinne, et al., 5181.

195 Smets, Tinne, et al., 5181.

196 Onwuteaka-Philipsen, Bregje D, et al. "Trends in end-of-life practices before and after the enactment of the euthanasia law in the Netherlands from 1990 to 2010: a repeated cross-sectional survey."

Made in the USA
Monee, IL
19 February 2020